modern readers — stage 2

Swallow Valley

Eduardo Amos
Elisabeth Prescher
Ernesto Pasqualin

2nd edition

Richmond

© EDUARDO AMOS, ELISABETH PRESCHER, ERNESTO PASQUALIN, 2005

Richmond

Diretoria: *Paul Berry*
Gerência editorial: *Sandra Possas*
Coordenação de revisão: *Estevam Vieira Lédo Jr.*
Coordenação de produção gráfica: *André Monteiro, Maria de Lourdes Rodrigues*
Coordenação de produção industrial: *Wilson Troque*

Projeto editorial: *Kylie Mackin*

Edição e preparação de texto: *Kylie Mackin*
Assistência editorial: *Gabriela Peixoto Vilanova*
Revisão: *Maria Cecília Kinker Caliendo*
Projeto gráfico de miolo e capa: *Ricardo Van Steen Comunicações e
 Propaganda Ltda./Oliver Fuchs*
Edição de arte: *Christiane Borin*
Ilustrações de miolo e capa: *Victor Tavares*
Diagramação: *Formato Comunicação*
Pré-impressão: *Helio P. de Souza Filho, Marcio H. Kamoto*
Impressão e acabamento: *Coan Indústria Gráfica Ltda.*
Lote: *278437*

**Dados Internacionais de Catalogação na Publicação (CIP)
(Câmara Brasileira do Livro, SP, Brasil)**

Amos, Eduardo
 Swallow valley / Eduardo Amos, Elisabeth Prescher,
Ernesto Pasqualin. 2. ed. — São Paulo : Moderna, 2004 —
(Modern readers ; stage 2)

 1. Inglês (Ensino fundamental) I. Prescher,
Elisabeth. II Pasqualin, Ernesto. III. Título. IV. Série.

04-0931   CDD-372.652

Índices para catálogo sistemático:
1. Inglês : Ensino fundamental   372.652

ISBN 85-16-04091-7

Reprodução proibida. Art. 184 do Código Penal e Lei 9.610 de 19 de fevereiro de 1998.

Todos os direitos reservados.

RICHMOND
EDITORA MODERNA LTDA.
Rua Padre Adelino, 758 — Belenzinho
São Paulo — SP — Brasil — CEP 03303-904
Central de atendimento ao usuário: 0800 771 8181
www.richmond.com.br
2019

Impresso no Brasil

Chapter 1

MILLERSVILLE DAILY NEWS
Tuesday, August 21

Local Teacher Wins National Award

Science teacher, Laura Higgs, will receive a special award from the National Green Association, a non-governmental organization for the protection of nature.

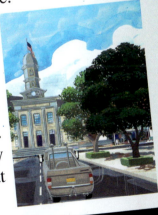

The award is for her work protecting the old oak trees on Sunset Avenue. Thanks to her, progress and nature grow side by side in our town.

The award ceremony will take place tonight at City Hall.

News from City Hall

Don't miss "Chat with the Mayor" tonight, at 9:30 on Channel 8. Mayor Cummings promises important news for our community!

3

Millersville is a small town near Highway 77. The two main industries are tourism and farming – wheat and corn.

Tourists usually come to Millersville to see the old water mill on Silver Creek. The mill is from the time of the first farmers in the region. Tourists can swim in the creek and enjoy a peaceful day in the park.

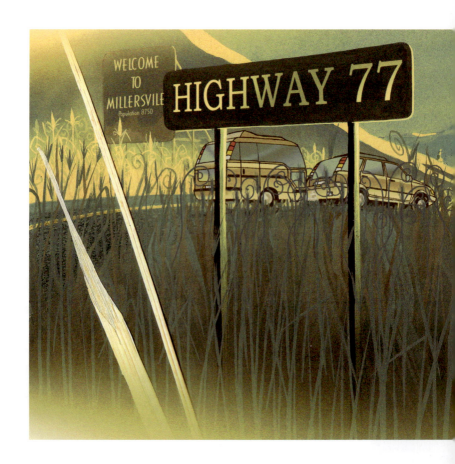

Millersville is also famous for Swallow Valley. In summer, thousands of swallows come to the valley to build their nests. Their visit attracts tourists from many different places.

 ## Chapter 2

Mayor Cummings – Good evening, citizens of Millersville. Let's begin our "Chat with the Mayor". But, first of all, my congratulations to Laura Higgs for her award.

Now, I want to introduce Mr Gordon Blake, president of the Star Tech Company. He has very important news for our community. Good evening, Mr Blake.

Gordon Blake – Good evening, Mayor Cummings, and good evening to the people of Millersville. I am the president of Star Tech, one of the biggest computer parts companies in the country. Star Tech is expanding now and we want to build a plant here in Millersville.

Mayor Cummings – But why in Millersville?

Gordon Blake – Because we are increasing production and we are going to need good transportation. Millersville is very close to Highway 77. This is important for us.

Mayor Cummings – But how is the plant going to benefit our town?

Gordon Blake – First of all, new jobs: 150 new jobs for young people. And a lot of tax money for the city.

Mayor Cummings – That's good news. Many young people are unemployed in our town. They need jobs. And we can use the tax money to build a new hospital and a new bus station. We can improve our streets too.

Gordon Blake – But that's not all. The company is going to build a large community center in Swallow Valley. The center is going to have swimming pools, basketball, volleyball and tennis courts, a playground, and a restaurant.

Mayor Cummings – Well, citizens of Millersville. That is tonight's news. Progress is finally coming to our town.

Chapter 3

On Wednesday morning, everybody in town is excited. At Millersville High School, the students are talking about the Star Tech project. Some of the older kids want to do computing courses. They want to work for Star Tech in the future. And some of the teachers are talking about the computers that the company is going to donate to the school and the city library.

Everybody is excited about the new community center.

When the bell rings, the students go to their classrooms. The *7th graders are restless. They are waiting for their first class. It is science, and Mrs Higgs is their teacher.

Mrs Higgs – You're all so excited this morning. What's going on, kids?

Martha – We are talking about the new company in Millersville, Mrs Higgs.

Ricky – The Star Tech project.

---

* 7th grade in the USA = 6ª série no Brasil

Mrs Higgs – What do you think about it?

Ricky – I think it's good. We need new jobs. My brother Gary has to go to Stoneburg to work. There is no work for him in Millersville.

Marion – That's true. There's no work for young people here. My sister is a data processor and she has to travel to Stoneburg every day.

Mrs Higgs – You are right. We need more jobs for young people here in Millersville.

Mrs Higgs – But what about Swallow Valley? They are going to take it from us.

Helen – Yes, but they are going to build a big community center, Mrs Higgs.

Mrs Higgs – But can a community center compensate for the loss of the valley?

Helen – What do you mean?

Mrs Higgs – Well, let's think. What do we have in Swallow Valley?

Ricky – The swallows.

Frank – Thousands of swallows come here in the summer.

Marion – ...and the tourists. The tourists come here to see the swallows in the valley.

Mrs Higgs – What else is important for our town?

Martha – The mill. The water mill on Silver Creek.

Ricky – Yeah, I like to swim there on weekends.

Mrs Higgs – I know, but the mill is also important for our town. Do you remember why?

Helen – I do, Mrs Higgs. The mill is part of our history. Millersville is the city of the millers.

Ricky – Are they going to destroy the mill?

Mrs Higgs – Yes, and the valley, too. They are going to build their new plant on the west side of the creek.

Frank – But that's where Swallow Valley is!

The students are surprised and angry. They don't want to lose the valley and the mill.

The 7th graders call all the other students and the teachers for a special meeting after school.

They discuss the advantages and disadvantages of the new plant. They think that it is important for the people of Millersville. On the other hand, they don't want to lose Swallow Valley.

After a long discussion, they conclude that Star Tech shouldn't build their plant in Swallow Valley. They want the company to choose another area in Millersville.

The students decide to protest against the destruction of Swallow Valley. They paint protest signs and march to City Hall.

Chapter 4

One week later, the headline in the Millersville Daily News says...

MILLERSVILLE DAILY NEWS

Monday, August 27

Star Tech Project is at the Starting Gate

The project for the new plant is ready. Star Tech engineers and architects are already in town. Construction is going to start next Thursday.

PROTEST AGAINST DESTRUCTION OF SWALLOW VALLEY

Yesterday, the students from Millersville High School protested against the new Star Tech project. They marched to City Hall.

The students of Millersville High School are furious at the news. They decide to organize a community debate on the destruction of Swallow Valley.

Student 1 – We have to do something, Mrs Higgs!
Student 2 – Yes, but what?
Student 3 – Let's start a movement!
Mrs Higgs – Yes, that's a good idea. We can call it "Friends of Swallow Valley".
Everybody – Yes, let's!

On the same day, the new organization, Friends of Swallow Valley, prints pamphlets and distributes them around town. The Friends of Swallow Valley convince the community to fight for the preservation of the valley.

On Tuesday, there's a crowd in front of City Hall. Mrs Higgs, the head of the movement, leads the debate between the students and the rest of the community.

They decide to camp in the valley.

When the sun rises on Wednesday morning, there are tents all over Swallow Valley and hundreds of painted signs.

Star Tech trucks and tractors are in the valley. Soon, the police and company security guards arrive. They tell the campers to leave the area, but they refuse.

The tension in the valley is increasing. When the tractors start to advance, the people in the camp throw stones at them and shout, "Go away! Go away! We want our valley!"

All of a sudden, there is a shot.

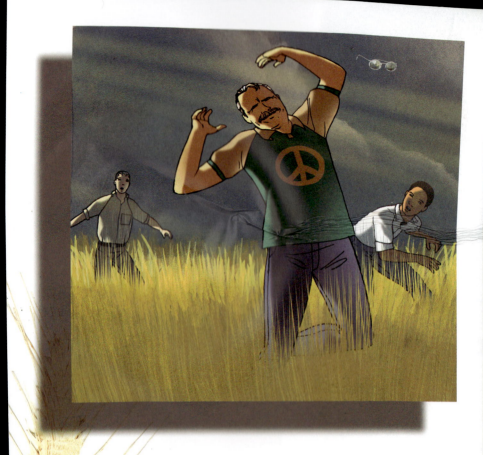

 # Chapter 5

Jeff Anderson, the Math teacher, is hurt. There is blood all over his shirt.

Soon, an ambulance is on the scene. Mr Anderson is soon on his way to hospital. The policemen and security guards also start to leave. The trucks and tractors drive away. Many campers leave, too. But some members of the movement stay. They want to protect Swallow Valley.

Mr Anderson doesn't recover from his wounds. And that same afternoon, he dies in hospital. Everyone is shocked.

That evening, there is tension and revolt on every street corner of Millersville.

Mr Anderson's funeral is on Thursday morning. Everybody goes to the graveyard. All the students are there to say their last good-byes to their teacher.

Mrs Higgs is very upset and moved. She makes a speech.

"Violence is not the way to solve problems. We have to talk. We have to find a peaceful way to solve our problems. We have to try. We owe it to Mr Anderson. I propose that Star Tech, the Mayor, and a group of people from the community sit down together, discuss the issues, and find a solution."

Two days later, the City Hall auditorium is packed. At the table on the stage, are Mayor Cummings, Gordon Blake, and a group of Millersville residents.

The residents talk about the importance of Swallow Valley.

Mr Blake – I understand your point of view. It is clear to me now. But you have to understand that we need good, efficient transportation. It is very simple. We want to build our factory in the valley because it is near Highway 77.

Mayor Cummings – Let's look carefully at the map of Millersville. Maybe we can find another area for the plant.

They look at the map and try to identify possible locations for the new plant on the other side of the city.

Mr Blake – The roads on that side of town are very bad. Star Tech doesn't have the money to spend on a new road. I think the project is impossible there.

Mrs Higgs – Wait! I think there is a way. The real problem is money, isn't it? Can't we use the City Emergency Fund to build the road?

Mayor Cummings – But there isn't enough money in the fund, Mrs Higgs. We need more money!

Everybody starts debating. Many people want to give their opinions. After some time…

Mrs Higgs – The citizens want to help too. We can give up the new Community Center. Star Tech can use the money from the Community Center to help build the new road. What do you think, Mr Blake? Do you agree?

There is silence in the audience. Mr Blake thinks for a while and then he says.

Mr Blake – I admire what you are doing... and I agree! With your help, I think the company can spend a little more. Then, we can build the road.

Everybody starts shouting and clapping.

Thanks to a common effort, Swallow Valley is safe. Progress is not going to destroy nature and history in Millersville!

KEY WORDS

The meaning of each word corresponds to its use in the context of the story (see page number 00)

advance (21) avanço
advantage (15) vantagem
against (15) contra
award (3) prêmio
bell (10) sinal, sino
benefit (7) beneficiar
blood (22) sangue
camp (19) acampar
camper (20) campista
carefully (25) cuidadosamente
choose (15) escolher
citizen (8) cidadão
clap, clapping (26) bater palmas
close (7) perto
compensate (12) compensar
computing course (9) computação, curso de informática
conclude (15) concluir
convince (18) convencer
corn (4) milho
court (8) corte
creek (4) riacho, córrego
crowd (19) multidão
data processor (11) digitador
disadvantage (15) desvantagem
donate (9) doar

else (13) mais
effort (27) esforço
expanding (6) expandir
farmer (4) fazendeiro
farming (4) agricultura, lavoura
furious (17) furioso
graveyard (24) cemitério
grow (3) crescer
headline (16) manchete
head (19) líder
hundreds (19) centenas
issue (24) problema, tópico
improve (6) melhorar
increase, increasing (7) aumentar
lead, leads (19) guiar, conduzir
library (9) biblioteca
loss (12) perda
main (4) principal
march (15) marchar
mayor (6) prefeito
miller (13) pessoa que trabalha no moinho ou engenho
movement (17) movimento
nest (5) ninho
non-governmental (3) não-governamental
oak (3) carvalho

owe (24) dever
packed (25) lotado
peaceful (4) pacífico
plant (6) fábrica
print, prints (18) imprimir
receive (3) receber
recover (23) recuperar
refuse (20) recusar
resident (25) morador
restless (10) impaciente
rise, rises (19) levantar
safe (27) seguro
security guard (20) segurança
shot (21) tiro
side (14) lado
sign (15) cartaz
soon (22) logo
stage (25) palco
swallow (5) andorinha
tax money (7) dinheiro de
imposto
tent (19) barraca
thousands (5) milhares
throw (21) jogar, atirar
town (4) cidade

truck (20) caminhão
true (11) verdade
upset (24) triste
unemployed (8)
desempregado
valley (5) vale
water mill (4) moinho de água
west (14) oeste
wheat (4) trigo
wound (23) machucado,
ferida

Expressions

All of a sudden (21) De
repente
drive away (22) ir embora
first of all (6) primeiramente
for a while (26) por um tempo
Go away! (21) Vá embora!
On the other hand (15) Por
outro lado
side by side (3) lado a lado
take place (3) acontecer
What's going on? (10) O que
está acontecendo?

ACTIVITIES

Before Reading

1. What can you do to protect nature?
2. Circle the words you think are going to appear in the story, according to the title and the cover of the book.

> true   ocean   school   flower   water   nature
> company   bird   city   restaurant   airplane   sun

While Reading

Chapter 1

3. Unscramble the letters to form words that are in the newspaper on page 3.
   R W A R D A _____
   U T E R A N _____
   K A O _____
   N E M Y C R E O _____
   H A T C R E E _____
   E N R E G _____

4. Answer the questions.
   1) What is the name of the town?
   2) What are the main industries?
   3) How old is the mill?
   4) What can tourists do in this town?

Chapter 2

5. What will be the new things in the town after the plant is built? Check page 8.

6. Write T for the true sentences and F for the false sentences.

a) (   ) Gordon Blake is the president of the country.
b) (   ) Star Tech is one of the biggest computer parts companies.
c) (   ) Millersville is close to Highway 77.
d) (   ) Many young people work in Millersville.
e) (   ) There's a big community center in Swallow Valley.
f) (   ) Mayor Cummings thinks progress is coming to Millersville.

Chapter 3

7. What are people talking about? Why are they excited?

8. Match the questions to the answers below.

a) What's going on, kids?
b) What do you think about it?
c) What do we have in Swallow Valley?
d) What else is important for our town?
e) Are they going to destroy the mill?

(   ) The mill.
(   ) We are talking about the new company.
(   ) Yes, and the valley, too.
(   ) I think it's good.
(   ) The swallows.

9. The students decide to protest against the destruction of Swallow Valley. Why? What do they do?

Chapter 4

10. Use the words below to complete the sentences.

> tension   plant   movement   protested   marched

a) The project for the new _____ is ready.
b) Students _____ against the new project.
c) They _____ to City Hall.
d) There is _____ and revolt.
e) Let's start a _____!

11. What's the name of the movement? What did they convince the community to do?

12. What's in the valley? Write words using the letters below.

T R __ __ __
T R A __ __ __ __
P O __ __ __ __
S E __ __ __ __ __ __   G U __ __ __ __
C A __ __ __ __ __

Chapter 5

13. Word search.

B T E E C L L C D I O F K A Z
H Z L K G X F A Y N T A M F Q
M E B D B Y D N R R U B I Y N
D R A Y E V A R G E U O B R A
N Q T N T P T T S L N L W O T
W L O T M T Y I A T O U C T U
S M I O R T C N Q O R N F C R
A D C J I E C I D W P E B A E
N W S I L E N C E D C W E F X
K C U R T B J H H L M A P T E

> ambulance   blood   company   factory   funeral
> graveyard   map   money   nature
> silence   street   table   truck   wound

After Reading (Optional Activities)

14. What do you think about what the kids did? Do you think this is the right way of solving this kind of conflict?

15. Choose something in the environment where or near where you live which has an environmental problem and try to think of some solutions.

16. "Preservation" versus "Progress". Hold a class debate.